Tedburn St Mary

Lilian Woolnough

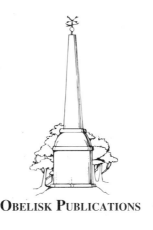

OBELISK PUBLICATIONS

OTHER OBELISK PUBLICATIONS

Around & About The Haldon Hills – Revisited, *Chips Barber*
The Lost City of Exeter – Revisited, *Chips Barber*
Diary of a Dartmoor Walker, *Chips Barber*
Diary of a Devonshire Walker, *Chips Barber*
The Great Little Dartmoor Book, *Chips Barber*
Made in Devon, *Chips Barber and David FitzGerald*
Haunted Pubs in Devon, *Sally and Chips Barber*
Dark & Dastardly Dartmoor, *Sally and Chips Barber*
Weird & Wonderful Dartmoor, *Sally and Chips Barber*
Ghastly & Ghostly Devon, *Sally and Chips Barber*
The Dartmoor Quiz Book, *Chips Barber*
Ten Family Walks on Dartmoor, *Sally and Chips Barber*
Six Short Pub Walks on Dartmoor, *Sally and Chips Barber*
Colourful Dartmoor, *Chips Barber*
Railways on and Around Dartmoor, *Chips Barber*
Devon's Railways of Yesteryear, *Chips Barber*
Place-Names in Devon, *Chips Barber*
An A–Z of Devon Dialect, *Chips Barber*
Street-names of Exeter, *Mary Ruth Raymond*

*We have over 170 Devon-based titles; for a list of current books please send SAE to
2 Church Hill, Pinhoe, Exeter, EX4 9ER or telephone (01392) 468556*

Acknowledgements

Thanks to Ernie Woolnough, June Redfern, James Gibbs, Christine Martin, Peter Bromell,
and to those who have given me their every support.
All pictures collected or supplied by the author
apart from pages 6, 19, 31 and 32 by Chips Barber
and page 28 by Francis Cann.

*First published in 2001 by
Obelisk Publications, 2 Church Hill, Pinhoe, Exeter, Devon
Designed and Typeset by Sally Barber
Printed in Great Britain
by Colour C, Tiverton, Devon*

© Lilian Woolnough/Obelisk Publications 2001

Tedburn St Mary

Tedburn St Mary

Introduction

It will be obvious to the reader that this is not a comprehensive history of the village: it is more of a general introduction to Tedburn's past. It has been compiled from information gathered over quite a period of time from a number of sources. It is hoped that this will satisfy the 'average' reader by providing a little more information than the knowledge they might have already acquired about the village. I also hope that it will spur a few others to become involved in more detailed research on topics which capture their imagination.

What's in a Name?

At the time of the Domesday Book (1086) our village was entered as 'Tetborne'. It would seem that with the building of the parish church in the thirteenth century, it acquired St Mary as an appendage to its name. A map of 1575 records it as St Marytetborne. Of the several theories proposed regarding the origins of the name, the most easily acceptable, and probably the correct one, is that it simply refers to the River Ted.

Polwhele's *History of Devonshire* (1793–1806) notes that the name comprises a combination of the British word 'tywood', which means 'sand', and the Saxon word 'burn', which means 'watercourse'. In the fullness of time,'Tywoodburn' was shortened down to 'Tedburn', which might mean 'Sandbrook'. Another local history reference, Lysons' *Magna Britannia* (Devon, 1822), suggests that Tedburn got its name from the Devonshire custom of burning the soil before tillage.

The original village was situated in and around the parish church; the cluster of houses still grouped there is evidence of this. What we now consider to be the centre of the village was known as 'Taphouse', referring to an inn at the crossroads where the Crediton and Exeter roads meet. In 1356 it was recorded as 'La Taphouse'. With the village store and the King's Arms still located on this crossroads, it was Taphouse which eventually came to be called Tedburn St Mary.

Polwhele recorded the earliest population figure for Tedburn in the period between 1793 and 1806, when *the inhabitants, about 200, are said to be remarkable for health, strength and longevity and are mostly employed in agriculture and spinning. There are rack-holders, lease holders and freeholders – and commonly about 30 paupers.*

In 1851 (by which time the population had risen to 861) 35 farmers were listed, and some of their names will 'ring a bell' with long-standing inhabitants of the village: John Henry of Melhuish, George Hodge Jnr of Upcott, Henry Priston of Upcott, Thomas Saffin of Higher Town and John Stanbury. Also listed were: three beer houses; three boot and shoemakers; two bricklayers; two blacksmiths – John Lake and John Marchant; eight carpenters including George Milford, Henry Pook and John Priston; two shopkeepers – Daniel Marchant and William Wills; and three tailors – John Milford, William Morrish and Richard Parsons.

The Parish Church

The Parish Church dates from the thirteenth century. *Kelly's Directory* of 1914 states that: *It is a building of red sandstone and consists of chancel, nave, north aisle, south porch and a western tower with pinnacles – containing six bells, dates respectively 1821 (1) 1717 (2 and 3) 1770 (4 and 5) and the tenor 1837 (6).*

The chancel is early English but the nave and north aisle are of a later date. On the south side it is a Chantry chapel. The chancel was rebuilt, and the nave restored and re-seated, in 1868.

A brass memorial tablet to Dr Edward Gee, a former Rector who died in 1618, was removed from the chancel during the restoration and replaced in 1914 in the West end of the nave. There are 200 sittings. The register of baptisms dates from the year 1558, marriages 1653 and burials 1689.

In notes from Mr H. Fulford Williams' 1965 thesis on Tedburn St Mary, we learn that the first recorded rector was Robert le Dun, who was installed in 1266. Another interesting detail to emerge is that "the Rev Edward Gee installed in 1596 got badly into debt and did duty on Sundays and always slept in the sanctuary of the church where he could not be arrested for debt under the then laws". Other rectors included Charles Burns, who had been chaplain aboard HMS *Neptune* at the Battle of Trafalgar in 1805. He died in 1852.

When the church was re-floored in 1868, nine large skeletons were found laid at no great depth. They were all some six feet in height and appear to have been buried at the same time. There is no clue to their identity and they have since been reburied at a greater depth.

School room

Many people will have noticed a small building to the left of the path leading to the Parish Church. This charming two-storey edifice is the old school room. Regrettably now in some state of dereliction, this used to house a dame school on the first floor. Underneath there was a stable for the rector to tether his horse! There are plans to restore this period building but funds are limited.

Methodist Church

It is believed that John Wesley slept at Colley Hayes on his way to Cornwall. Mrs Lambert Dennis, in an excellently written history of the Methodist Church at Tedburn, recalls Granny Roynon, a local character who, in difficult times, trudged many a weary mile to collect money to liquidate the debt on the chapel. It was mainly her zeal that kept it open.

By 1928 the church was growing in numbers and influence and it was felt that the time had come to arise and build a more substantial place of worship. After considerable trouble, an excellent site was secured on the Fulford estate, close to the old building. But funds were urgently required. A generous grant from the National Methodist body (Connexion) was received to guarantee the project and more than £380 was raised by staging three garden parties. By the time the building was commenced, the noble sum of £1,400 had been realised. The foundation stones were laid on 31 July 1929. The work proceeded satisfactorily until a fearful storm in the following December brought down the front gable. However, the builders carried on and made good to produce the fine building which stands today.

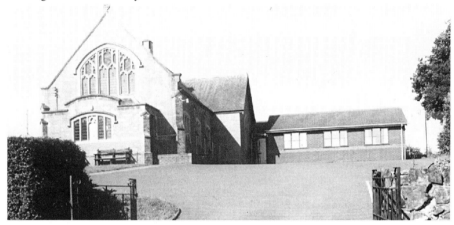

In the aforementioned front gable, there is a beautiful window which is thought to be a gift from Mr Charles Slade to the memory of his mother, who was a devoted member of the church. The oak seats, now outside the present chapel, were dedicated to the same Mrs Slade, who was born in Tedburn 1854 and whose family lived at Odhams Cottage, Winslake Foot.

The Methodist School Room

I am grateful to Roger Thorne for providing these details. There is some uncertainty about the date of the former chapel (later Sunday school, now a dwelling). It seems to have been converted from cottages about 1859 and used until the present chapel was built in 1930. The 1859 building was Free Methodist (a division from the Wesleyans), whilst the 1930 building was United Methodists. At Halstow Farm in the parish of Dunsford, the Wesleyans had a chapel, which is now a barn. Opened about 1840 and closed in about 1885, it was too far from the village to survive. The Wesleyans were unable to get a more suitable site as the Fulfords owned most of the land. A number of houses were licensed for Wesleyan services in the period 1816–1842. The original certificates are kept at the Devon Record Office in Exeter.

Here is an extract from the former *Devon & Exeter Gazette.*

The story of Methodism in the Tedburn St Mary district where a new church was opened yesterday, goes back to the beginning of the nineteenth century though it was not until 1840 that Tedburn actually appeared on the Plan of the Exeter Wesleyan Circuit and a chapel was built at Halstow, two miles from the village. The earliest record of Methodist preaching in the neighbourhood is probably that which took place at Crediton (only four miles distant) in 1790 just a year or so before the death of John Wesley himself. Wesley, by the by, is believed to have been a fairly familiar figure to the neighbourhood, passing on horseback as he must have done

Tedburn St Mary

during his journeys in the West Country. In those early days at Halstow the cause was dependent largely upon two farmers. By today the old chapel which still stands has become a farmhouse barn, a tragic sequel to the great disruption of 1847 at Halstow, the effects of which were felt even

in the most remote localities, and a resolution which appears in a minute book of the Exeter Reformers under the date October 31st 1851 may be cited as the origin of the Free Methodist cause at Tedburn. The resolution instructed "Brother Jarman" to make "the necessary enquiries with references to a room at Taphouse for holding a reform meeting there". That meeting in fact was held in a cottage occupied by a Mrs Kelly in the centre of the hamlet, and later in a cottage of a Mrs Lake of Colley Hayes. The movement must have grown fairly rapidly for by the next year the congregations were said to average from 110 to 120 and services were held not only twice on Sunday but also each Wednesday night.

The Chapel of Rest

The cemetery adjoining the Chapel of Rest was formed in 1886. Of this, a portion was consecrated by the Bishop of Crediton in 1904 and is under the control of the Parish Council as Burial Board. However, in recent years a separate committee approved by the Parish Council has undertaken the restoration of the Chapel itself, which otherwise might not have survived. They meet regularly to discuss fund-raising and the progress of the restoration. The bell-tower recently having been made safe, the chapel bell was rung for the first time in many years at the carol concert in December 1992.

A number of the village residents have visited the Chapel and have written to say how delighted they are that a valuable piece of village history has been maintained.

Tedburn St Mary 1660–1714

Fortunately a few interesting snippets of local history remain from this time. They mainly revolve around the so-called Monmouth Rebellion and the Parish Church.

Charles II became King with the Restoration of the Monarchy in 1660. Following the King's death in 1685, his illegitimate son, the Duke of Monmouth, attempted to claim the throne for himself. This uprising against James II was known as The Monmouth Rebellion, but was only supported by yeomen, clothiers and miners in the South West of England; it lacked the powerful backing of society on a national scale. James's reaction was to confront the Duke of Monmouth at Sedgemoor in Somerset. This was the last great battle on English soil and one in which the King's forces triumphed. Those rebels who survived the bloody conflict fled, but were hounded down. Many were brought before the ruthless Judge Jeffreys; the severity of the sentencing led to these trials being known as 'The Bloody Assizes'.

Tedburn was known to have been slightly involved: whilst in the village, Lt Clarke is noted as having 'written a rate' for it on behalf of James II.

In 1692 John Tippett, a local man, was paid 16s 6d for eleven days' wages as a soldier against the French. This can be compared to the 9s 8d paid for 7lbs of powder and 8lbs of ball. Nine years earlier, William Hay was paid 4s for pulling ivy from the walls of the church, whilst Elizabeth Hay received 4s for sweeping the church for a whole year!

Local Inns

The King's Arms Inn dates back to the early 1600s. After the English Civil War (1642–1646) it was known as The Taphouse Inn. It is believed that Charles II called here whilst on his way to Cornwall and that this visit brought about the name change to the King's Arms. During the

nineteenth century, improvements to the road and an increase in travellers helped to make the inn a prosperous and busy place. It is still an inn of great attraction, having lost little of its former glory.

It has had many colourful landlords. Mr William Miller, who passed away in the 1920s, was landlord for an unbroken spell of 50 years. He died at the inn in his 80th year. He was also a vendor of seeds and fertilisers and an expert on agriculture. His advice was much sought, not only in the district but also across the county. His funeral was attended by a large and representative gathering from this and many surrounding parishes.

Mrs Miller is featured in this picture, where the sign on the wall stated that "Bus passengers may wait in the dining room". Would that bus passengers enjoyed such privilege today! Mr and Mrs Miller were the grandparents of Donald and Raymond Miller.

For many years members of William's family managed the well-known Miller's Hatcheries in Tedburn, which gave employment to a good number of local people.

The Red Lion, on the opposite side of the main road, is also a well-established place of refreshment. Unfortunately I have been unable to trace any of its early history.

Tedburn Fair

The origins of the annnual fair go back a long way. Polwhele's *History of Devonshire* states: "They have a wake or revel once a year", while in Lysons' *Britannia* it says that: "There is a cattle fair on the Monday before Michaelmas Day".

The fair was not continued throughout the ages – there were periods when it lapsed. It was reinstated at the beginning of the twentieth century. In the year 2000, the village staged the modern version with the 96th Fair and Sports event.

Some locals have memories of past events. Aubrey Dinnis recalled the fair of old, when there was a cattle and sheep market on the Monday, followed the next day with horse, sports and pleasure events. He also remembered the swing boats, which were a popular attraction with youngsters. The proceedings were rounded off on the Tuesday night when a dance was held in the schoolroom. The local lads would sing traditional country songs whilst Mr Milford and his son would play the piano and violin for dancing.

Donald Miller remembered fairs of the 1920s, when stalls in the village street sold wonderful gingerbread and home-made sweets. The pubs were open all day, which was almost a novelty in those times.

Today our fair is organised by a hard-working committee and features a craft tent, competitions, side-shows, clay-pigeon shooting, horse show, dog show and many other attractions.

Victorian Tedburn

In 1873 villagers were informed that soon there might be a State or Board School opening in Tedburn, as the Education Department deemed that one was necessary. Prior to this there had been a Parochial School, which operated from 1839 to the late 1860s; a Subscription School; and various Dame Schools, which were conducted in private houses around the village. Billing's *Directory* of 1857 reveals a few more details. It states that: *There is a small School for Boys supported by subscription and the children's payments. Mr W. Preston, Master, number of scholars – 25. There is also a Subscription School at Taphouse, number of scholars – 40, Jane Davies, Mistress.*

As for the Dame Schools, there are known to have been at least nine in existence in 1840. These establishments were generally believed to have been below the standards set by Her Majesty's Inspectors. Interestingly, Mrs Holman's Private School at North Park Lodge continued to operate until at least 1881, even though the State School had opened in 1877. The first Headmaster of this State School was Mr Pattinson, who lasted only a year. It later transpired that his certificate to teach was withdrawn by the Education Department. This decision appears to be justified: not only did he take his leave of the school; he also left with the school fees and the stationery which had been collected. It was an inauspicious start for the school but it added some spice to conversations around the village!

So far, the longest span of years spent at the helm belongs to Mr Pattinson's successor, who took over in 1878 and stayed until 1919. Mr A. J. Walters was the Head for 41 years! In a much changed world of education, his feat cannot be matched. From the details given below, a number of Heads gave about fifteen years of service.

The other Head teachers to date are as follows: Mr F. T. Eastwick (1920), Mr S. G. Westlake (1920–1935), Mr A. J. Sparks (1935–1939), Mr H. Parsons (1939–1945), Miss H. Mills (1945–1959), Mr J. Morrish (1959–1974), Miss J. Merrett (temporary 1974), Mr R. Lawrence (1974–1979), Mrs J. Welsh (acting head 1979–1980), Mr C. Impey (1980–1997). In 2001, at the time of writing, the Head is Mrs Debbie Buckingham.

Here we have the Tedburn St Mary County Primary School soccer team of the 1965/66 season. Back row, L to R: C. Putt, C. Adams, R. Matthews, S. Blake, I. Russell, R. Parsons, M. Bowden. Front row, L to R: R. Selley, D. Sheppard, N. Bromell and P. Lee.

In this next photograph we have Tedburn pupils from about 1957/58. The Headmistress, Miss Mills, is featured in the picture.

In 1977, when Tedburn St Mary Primary School celebrated its centenary, a booklet was produced to commemorate the event. It included these three photographs showing two classes from the 1920s, courtesy of Mrs N. Moore (formerly Miss Howard), and the school in 1977, courtesy of Mr K. Vincent of Christow.

The school celebrated its centenary in style – all the pupils donned Victorian dress for an event, which was blessed with fine weather.

County directories of the past provide further details of the village. White's *Directory* of 1850 includes the following: *Tedburn St Mary, a pleasant village on the Okehampton Road, 7½ miles W and N of Exeter has in its parish 867 souls and 4433 acres of land, generally fertile and hilly. It has a cattle fair on the Monday before Michaelmas Day and includes the hamlet of Upcott and many scattered farmhouses. At Domesday Survey, Tedbourne (Teteborne) was held by Ralph de Pomerai under Baldwin de Sap. It is now held by John Hippesley Esq. The manors of Hackworthy and Melhuish were formerly held by families of their own names and now belong to Baldwin Fulford Esq. of Fulford House ... John Abbot Esq. and several smaller owners have estates in the parish.*

More detail was included in the Kelly's *Directory* entry for the village in 1856: *Baldwin Fulford Esq. and John Henry Hippesley are Lords of the Manor and with Miss Abbot are the chief landowners.* The 'gentry' are listed as Thomas Batson Esq. of Colley House, Rev Charles Burne (Rector), Mrs Elizabeth Burne of Thornwood House and the Rev J. W. T. Lee, curate, of the Rectory. So Tedburn could sport four gentry in 1856. This directory emphasises the class distinction which was prevalent then, as traders were considered in a class of their own. The backbone of the community, they included 32 farmers, 11 carpenters, 2 thatchers, 2 bricklayers, 3 boot and shoe makers, 2 blacksmiths, 3 tailors, 1 wheelwright, 2 shopkeepers and 1 butcher. There were also William Davis, mason and postmaster; William Lethbridge, beer retailer; William May of the King's Arms; William Preston, master at the Free School; John Sandford of the Red Lion; and John Triggs, Parish Clerk.

The Hodge family appear to have figured largely in 1850. Three of them farmed at Uppacott, Great Huish and Lower Uppacott. A fourth member of the family was a carpenter.

Some names which appeared then are still familiar to local people: John Lake – blacksmith; Richard Parsons – tailor; Thomas Saffin – farmer at Higher Town; William Westcott – carpenter; Henry Pook – carpenter. Until the late 1980s, Miss Avis Pook still lived at Fairview. This house was built by her grandfather, John Pook, in 1870. By renting the Rectory Glebe, the Pooks ran a small dairy farm. They sold cream and milk from a room at the back of the house. This practice continued until the 1930s.

In 1850, William Lake was victualler of the King's Arms whilst Daniel Marchant performed the same role at the Red Lion. Tedburn then had three beer houses, so it would appear that no one needed to have remained thirsty!

Prior to 1821, the main road between Exeter and Okehampton lay along Okehampton Street and over the hills through Whitestone. On 21 January that year it was agreed to forge a new route between Pocombe Bridge and Tedburn. The earlier route was little more than a rough cart track. Mr D. J. Pike of Hill Farm, Whitestone, believed that the original route had so many bends and corners because it had to link with existing farm tracks and lanes. The new route, which followed valleys where possible, made for an easier journey.

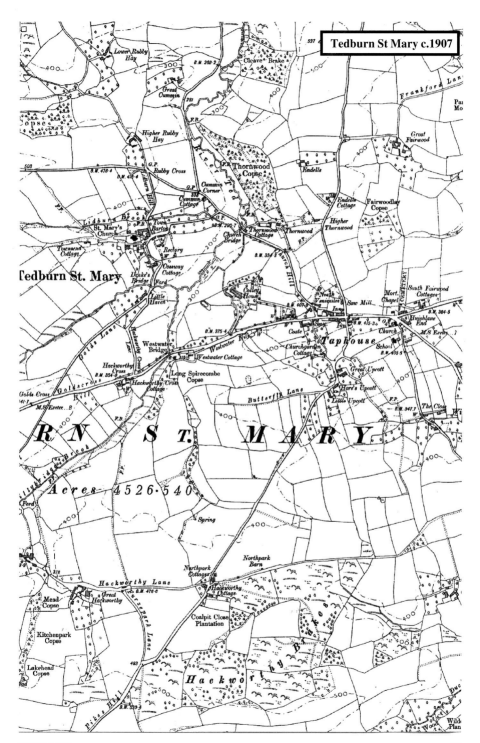

Tedburn St Mary c.1907

Despite being on a main route, transport was limited in the middle of the nineteenth century. The Times coach from Truro to Exeter passed through the village on Mondays, Wednesdays and Fridays at 7.30 p.m. The return journeys passed through on Tuesdays, Thursdays and Saturdays at 8 a.m.

There was the Hodge Omnibus, which also ran from Truro to Exeter. Five carriers passed through several times a week on their way to or from the county town. In 1850, the post came daily from Exeter. There still are two Victorian wall letterboxes in the village, one at North Park, the other on the Old Tithe Barn near the church.

For those early or late travellers, there were street lights, Mr Saunders being one of the lamplighters.

By 1857, 31 farmers were listed. Among their number were the following: John Battin (Lower Hockworthy), G. & S. Hodge (Great Huish), Thomas Holman (Lower Rubby Hay), Edward Kelly (Oak Farm), George Ledge (Town Barton), James Morrish (Westwater), Henry Preston (Hores Uppacott), William Seward (Frankford) and John Stoneman (Lower Rubby). In the Taphouse area lived Davie William, builder and postmaster; John Hamilton and John Lake, blacksmiths; three boot and shoe makers; and Richard Parsons, tailor. It is interesting to note that William May is listed as both victualler and shoemaker at the King's Arms. Of course all of these people have passed into history but by the very nature of their occupations it conjures up for us a picture of a Tedburn of yesteryear, a place which was self-sufficient.

More than half a century later, in 1914, worldwide changes were afoot as The Great War commenced. At that time Tedburn had 25 farmers listed and among them are several names whose descendants are with us today or, if they are not, are clearly remembered: William Bromell (Higher Rubhay), Richard Dennis (Wayland), Samuel Dennis (Town Barton), George Hawkins (Frankford), William Phillips, who was also a rate collector (Coate Farm), George Pook (Little Haven), William Seward (Higher Berry & Windout), William Taylor (Brook Farm) and William Stanbury – butcher and farmer. Other familiar names were: Samuel Fry – wheelwright, William Miller – landlord of King's Arms, John Parsons – shopkeeper and post office, Mrs Mary Pook – dairy, James Shilston – carpenter, Denis Taylor – mason, and David Thorne – boot and shoemaker.

This picture of hay gathering shows Bert Miller, who will be remembered by many villagers, with his father. It was probably taken just before the First World War.

We have two long-standing farming families who are still renowned for their cider making – Grays of Halstow and Bromells of Lower Uppacott. The late Sid Bromell, when he was a 12-year-old, would take a horse and cart all the way to Chagford with cider and return with empty barrels. He believed that there was once a quarry on the brow of the hill where Homeview stands on the Whitestone road.

These pictures show the cider press at Lower Uppacott. In the picture above (from left to right) we have John Bromell, Sid Bromell, George Bromell, Percy Bromell, Henry Hall and Colin Wroth. Below, Percy Bromell raises a glass of cider.

A cider press was restored and placed beside the road to acknowledge the importance of this traditional drink.

When French prisoners-of-war were held at Princetown's war depot, cider was taken there from Halstow. As part payment for the heady liquor, granite posts and coping stones were brought back to the farm on the return journeys. Until the 1960s, records of receipts issued by British officers on duty on the Moor were held at Halstow.

The 1920s

This was a difficult decade for the country as a whole and there were also a few highs and lows for Tedburn. This appeared in the press on 6 August 1925: *Tedburn St Mary has the privilege of being able to claim Captain Donald Bellew as its Victoria Cross hero, for he lived here from infancy until he became a soldier. During the Great War a gallant defence of his gun almost single-handed and a refusal to surrender to overwhelming odds won him the Victoria Cross. Captain Bellew visited Tedburn last week when his old friends and neighbours cordially welcomed him and expressed their pride in the distinction he had gained.*

One of the most important village events of this decade was the opening of the first Village Hall. The *Devon & Exeter Gazette* reported the event on 29 November 1929: *Tedburn St Mary was en fête yesterday, when the new Village Hall was opened and sports were held. The Hall, which has been erected chiefly through the efforts of the Women's Institute, has a seating capacity of 200. The committee responsible for the erection of the new building were Messrs S. Miller, Stanbury, Ashworth, Cuddeford, Lendon and Hall and they were assisted by members of the W.I. The opening ceremony was performed by Captain Gatliff (Chairman of the Committee) who said the hall would meet a long-felt need, and he appealed to everyone to assist the committee to obtain the necessary furnishings. Following the ceremony about 120 sat down to luncheon in the new building. Music was provided by the Exeter Cadet Battalion Band.*

Here we have some old picture postcard views of the village. The best way to appreciate them is to stand on the spot where the photographer stood all those years ago and compare them with the present scene.

In this scene it has been raining and the tyre marks on the road are all too obvious. It also appears that a number of animals have also passed this way… The petrol pump on the right hand side belonged to Mr Fry's business. The building between the King's Arms and Fairview has since disappeared, to be replaced by the entrance to the King's Arms car park. It is likely that the carrier leading the horse (centre) is Mr Mudge, who is mentioned later.

The King's Arms is shown above opposite Tremlett's Cottages. At the front left is the wall of Monkey House, so called because a tenant once owned a monkey. The house has been pulled down in recent years. Note the oil standard street lamp (right foreground) outside what is now the Village Stores.

In the view below the King's Arms appears on the right hand side. The building to the front left could have been the former Red Lion Cottage, or an outbuilding to the house on the left. In any case it has been demolished, probably in the early 1970s.

The former A30, the main road between Exeter and Okehampton, passes through the village. This picture looks towards Chapel Corner. Again, on the road there are deposits from passing horses!

Tedburn St Mary 1939–1945

During the Second World War the black-out was adhered to, as it was nationally. The following details are included with the help of Mrs Jo Courtier. Many Devon towns and villages took evacuees from London. Most of those who were billeted at Tedburn were from Fulham. This influx of children posed a few problems; the increasing numbers at the school meant that pupils had to sit three to a desk and it was necessary to import two additional teachers, who both came from London. The Chapel Sunday School Room on the corner of School Lane had to be used as an extra classroom for the Council School.

As Tedburn was then much more of a farming community, a number of prisoners of war were brought in to help work the farms. At first these were mainly Italians but later Germans added to the labour force. Their meagre daily food allowance consisted of a small tin of tea, a little corned beef and a piece of bread. The farmers, for whom they worked, would supplement this with a good meal. The extra meal gave them more energy so that they would work harder!

There were also quite a few Land Girls, members of the Women's Land Army, working in the district. Protecting the village, and our homeland, was the stalwart Tedburn St Mary Home Guard Unit, dear old 'Dad's Army'.

There was a searchlight battery a little way down the Whitestone road in a field belonging to Mr Dennis. Fortunately Tedburn was spared any bombing but one of our own aircraft crashed at Huish Farm.

Following the entry of the USA into the war, a great many American troops passed through Tedburn at different times.

During the war there was a great community spirit. No church bells were rung as these were held back in case of an invasion. Had this happened, they would have been rung to warn those out in the fields and away from any wireless set.

The Parish Council

In December 1894, a meeting was held in the Board Schoolroom to elect the first Parish Council to represent the village, under the new Local Government Act.

Here are some excerpts from the Parish Council Records for the time up to 1963.

14 June 1902 – The first item on this meeting's agenda was regarding the preparation of an Address to His Majesty King Edward VII in connection with the public celebration of the

Coronation in this Parish: "The sum of about £35 was voluntarily contributed which was sufficient to provide a good dinner for all the male parishioners above the age of 15 years, and a meat tea for the women and children in a substantial booth erected in a field behind the Red Lion Inn, which was kindly lent to the Committee for the occasion by Mr Samuel Preston. The services of the Tedburn String Band were engaged. Three arches were erected in the village and decorated with evergreens. A sum of £2 was put aside for the purchase of mugs and medals to be presented to the children attending the Board School."

2 August 1928 – A letter of reply from the School Managers re "Extension of Time for Entertainment" stated that they saw no reason for altering their previous decision not to allow the School to be used on any occasion after midnight. This was in reply to a letter sent after the April meeting stating "This Council requests that the School Managers should in future grant the use of the Schoolroom for entertainment up to 2 a.m., on all days when there is no school in attendance on the following day".

The Roaring Twenties had arrived in Tedburn!

22 May 1952 – The most important item on the agenda concerned the water supply and sewage scheme. Everyone was told it would be some considerable time before approval to a sewage scheme could be obtained. The old chestnut "owing to the present situation" was used again. The Clerk was asked to write again to the RDC stressing that no parish in the whole of St Thomas Rural District suffered so badly as Tedburn from shortage of water. The water shortage was to drag on interminably!

16 January 1956 – A letter from Devon County Education Committee stated that the charge for the Schoolroom for the Parish Council meetings had been increased to 3s 6d as from October 1955. This was costed out as 3s for the caretaker and 6d for the lighting!

8 June 1956 – Special meeting to consider a proposal for Public Street Lighting. A large number of parishioners attended. At a vote, there were only eight votes in favour.

10 January 1958 – Mrs Harris asked by letter if anything could be done regarding her garden fence, which was continually being damaged by passing motorists. She lived in Huish Cottages opposite the Old Schoolroom on the A30. It was suggested a red arrow or reflector be placed on the fence. Unfortunately the saga of "Mrs Harris's fence" went on for a number of years and was a standing joke introduced into each year's pantomime. Mrs Harris didn't mind!

2 October 1963 – Pandemonium re the sewage situation: all sorts of dreadful problems had occurred in School Lane. Things were so bad it was agreed that the Chairman should ring our MP and ask him to come out and meet the Council at the site to inspect the damage.

Things Remembered about Tedburn

This is a collection of miscellaneous memories which have been handed down. It is hoped that now they are in print they, or the people who have kindly passed them on, will not be forgotten.

Aubrey Dinnis was an active and highly respected villager. He remembered those days when Mrs Pook of Fairview sold gun cartridges for local shoots, and there were only three cars in the village. He had fond recollections of dances held in the Reading Room, which was located in the upper rooms of East View Cottage, almost opposite the Village Stores. A good time was had by all!

He also recalled the time when the surface of the River Exe was frozen and three Tedburn villagers showed their prowess as ice-skaters.

Alf Wilson of Oak Farm recalled the long 'crocodile' of children being escorted from the school to Colley House, where Miss Cuddiford gave them all hot cross buns. He remembered the famous A. J. Coles, a former schoolmaster who created that wonderful Devonshire character Jan Stewer. The entertainer once lived at Poole Farm whilst his last years were spent in one of the first caravan homes at Pathfinder Village, a short distance from Tedburn. Mr and Mrs Coles celebrated their diamond wedding anniversary there in 1961. On the evening of 18

August 1965, he was killed by a van whilst walking along the road at Ferndown in Dorset. He was 89 years old.

Mrs Joyce Finlinson, née Bromell and the sister of Peter and Eric, is part of a family who can trace their association with Tedburn back to 1798! Their mother was a member of the Lake family, who were in the village at the end of the eighteenth century. Many years ago, Thomas Lake was the blacksmith at the Old Forge.

Peter Bromell has always been a great supporter of all that concerns the village. This young dairyman was out on his rounds even on the Coronation Day of Elizabeth II. The difference on this occasion was that Joe, his faithful hard-working horse, was presented with a gleaming harness; the horse-drawn cart was beautifully decorated.

Arthur C. Priston was born in 1897, the same year Queen Victoria's Diamond Jubilee was celebrated the length and breadth of the kingdom. In 1985, whilst living in Wiltshire, he wrote a letter recalling his memories of the village and its surroundings from his Tedburn days. Here are some of the details which he recalled.

"My grandfather, Peter Priston, saddler and shoemaker, moved to Tedburn about 1880. He originally lived at Christow, where he had a contract to supply and repair the harness and special boots which the tin miners used. This was on Lord Exmouth's estate. About this time alluvial tin was found in Siam which, being easier to find and with much cheaper labour, meant that the mines at Christow and elsewhere in Devon and Cornwall became no longer viable.

"He purchased the Old Toll House in Tedburn, a thatch building which in about 1916 (after the death of my grandmother) was sold to a Mr Fry, whose family are still in business in the village, I believe. He altered the old building considerably. The old porch and thatch was removed. In my time the wooden porch had two seats and two round glass windows about 5 to 6 inches in diameter; my cousin and I used to play pirates, imagining the porch as a ship. Also, it possessed double stable doors. Mr Fry bought it to house one of his staff who married a Miss Betty or Lettie Parsons. I remember her well. She was a lively girl with auburn hair.

"The same building is now the Village Store. There was a well at the side of the building in a shed, of which my grandfather always kept the key in his pocket. He had visions of me falling into this supply of water and he took no chances. I recall it was very deep and the atmosphere being ill-lit was very gloomy.

Tedburn St. Mary, Post Office.

"There had been a board above the building with toll fees painted on it. This was removed by my grandfather and fixed to a building immediately opposite. Just why this was done I cannot say. I suppose it was felt it should be preserved.

"I also recall at the junction of the cross-roads at the corner there was a granite pillar with three-prong metal spike reminding me of the Prince of Wales feathers. It appears the carts turning the corner sharply demolished the wall on occasions, and the old gentleman got tired of this, but whether he placed it there, or if the local authorities did, I cannot say.

"Mr and Mrs Parsons, who lived at the Post Office, in the building which housed the Reading Room, later moved to the opposite side of the road. I know Mr Parsons owned or rented a field near the church, which I saw him scythe the grass for hay – indeed, I helped! I recall he took his lunch together with a small firkin of cider. He passed this to me to have a drink, but finding the firkin somewhat cumbersome, I poured more down my neck than my throat!

"The Fry family – at my time they were wheelwrights and general builders, they bought trees and sawed them into planks. There was always plenty of timber about. They also milked several cows and supplied my grandparents with milk. At the west end of the village there was a general store run by, I believe, a maiden lady by the name of Westmacott. I can still smell this 'Harrods of the City' paraffin, oil, soap, naptha and so on. All the memorable smells of an old village shop. She also sold baby clothes, reels of cotton and so on but nothing very grand or big. She was also a great purveyor of news, for whenever my grandmother or my mother visited the store it became the occasion for a long yap!

"I became friendly with a lad of my own age whose father farmed at the west end of 'Taphouse'. It was through him that I became acquainted with the facts of life. Seeing him drive two cows through the main street and enquiring where he was going he informed me he was taking a cow to a bull and invited me to go along with him – and so I learned that the story of babies and the gooseberry bush was all 'twaddle'. The name of this family was Phillips.

"In my early days there were no buildings between Toll House and the cemetery. I recall there was a shed or barn at the junction of the old Exeter Road and the new. This was full of teasels, the growing of which was a speciality of a farmer by the name of Andrews who lived locally. These teasels were eventually sent to Stroud in Gloucestershire for the combing of broadcloth.

"I well remember going to church one Sunday morning and the lady organist started the opening chords for the last hymn, when the organ gave a deep groan. Frantically she tried again but nothing happened except a protesting wail, whereupon the old gentleman whose job it was to hand pump the bellows woke up with a start, having fallen asleep. I can still see the contorted facial features of the organist.

"It was customary for my family to travel to Tedburn at least twice a year, sometimes three, Easter, mid-summer and occasionally at Christmas. After arriving at Exeter we would repair to the museum and later to the Cathedral, where my father, who could sleep at the drop of a hat, would leave me to look around whilst he took a nap. I would spend the time reading the plaques and the tombs. I should say that I knew more of the interior of the bulding than those living there!

"About 4 p.m. we repaired to an inn near Exe Bridge to pick up the carrier, a tarpaulin covered cart drawn by two horses in tandem. The outfit belonged to a Mr Mudge, the termini being at Exeter and Chagford, or it could have been Drewsteignton. Usually I sat up with him at the front. He was a cheerful character. Only once did I sit inside where the occupants were mostly ladies who chewed their meal into small pieces, and their neighbours into even smaller ones. We always stopped at an inn called Half Way House [Travellers' Rest] but what it was half way to I never knew. Then we negotiated Five Mile Hill where the horses really had to work for their living. The roads were made of stone not Macadam and it was either dusty or muddy. Indeed in 1913, the last time I visited as a boy, I took my bicycle, and going towards Exeter the dust must have been two inches deep and although it was downhill I had to pedal quite hard and eventually fell or slid off.

I entered Exeter looking as if I had passed through a flour mill. Later there was a bus or coach, I believe run by a firm called Tilling. To me it didn't have the glamour of Mr Mudge's carrier.

"About a long mile from Toll House going west, on the south side of the road, there is a cottage nestling in a hollow in which an old lady was said to have been murdered for the gain of a silver coin. The criminal was the last person to be publicly hanged in Exeter and also I believe in England. My maternal grandfather who lived in the Ashburton district went to view this execution, but at the last moment his nerve failed him and he returned home at the carnival spirit which seemed part of the gruesome experience."

About the time of these recollections Mrs Westcott (I believe that was her name) had a little general shop in one of St Mary's Cottages. She sold almost everything and was also a great source of local goings-on about the village. The sign over the door, which I have looked at through a magnifying glass, advertised "Lipton's Teas".

The Village Hall

On 23 November 1974 a spacious new Village Hall, costing £20,000, was officially opened. It brought to fruition seven years of effort by villagers in raising the money to pay for it. Mr A. Milne of Thornwood, who presented the additional land needed for the project, performed the opening ceremony. Mr John Bromell, Hall Chairman, said it was a great occasion in the history of Tedburn. The villagers began raising money in 1967, achieving their target of £1,000 per annum for seven consecutive years. Aided by various grants, they covered all but £2,700 of the cost. The special guest of honour at the opening ceremony was Mr Aubrey Dinnis, who had been on the Hall Committee since the 1920s.

On 6 June 1991 an extension to the Hall was opened. This was made possible by the Tedburn St Mary Locality Planning Team. The Department of Health and Social Services were anxious to move Health Services from the town to the locality. The Village Hall was chosen for this purpose. But the hall was fully booked; where could they be accommodated? The idea of building an extension was put to the Hall Committee and the Parish Council, who, as trustees of the Hall, would have to be guarantors for any loans. Initially the estimated cost was about £60,000 but the need for a new boiler house and heating system drove the figure up to about £68,000. There were some major grants and significant contributions from local organisations. These included Tedburn Methodist Church, Drama Group, Tremletts Close Residents, Cheriton Bishop Methodist Church, Fingle Glen Golf Club and Tedburn Parish Council. There were also a great many fund-raising events: strawberry teas, fêtes and fairs realised more than £4,000. Individual contributions added another £2,700 and interest-free loans put another £3,250 into the coffers. These loans were repaid within four years.

The hall has also received a new roof, £35,000 being required for this.

The next sequence of photographs shows just a small number of the many productions which have been staged in the Village Hall.

Five Crusaders front the cast of this production from 1967.

Above we have the cast of the 1971 production of *Sleeping Beauty*.
The picture of jolly hockey sticks and tennis comes from another lively 1970s production.

The scene above shows the glamour and glitter of a 1920s evening presented in 1976. In the same year there was also a production of *Bluebeard*: on stage below we have (from left to right) Kath Martin, Shirley Garrish and Stella Wilson.

In the early 1980s *Les Girls* (apart from one boy!) in Tedburn St Mary included Carrie Ann Bastin, Petrina Rivers, Rupert Vowler, Jane Vowler, Charlotte Vowler and Hayley Wood. *Puss in Boots* was chosen for the pantomime in 1987.

Ten years later, in 1997, the pantomime was *Ali Baba*.

The last picture of this sequence was taken outside the Village Hall and shows the smartly-attired Drum Majorettes. One has temporarily stepped out of line!

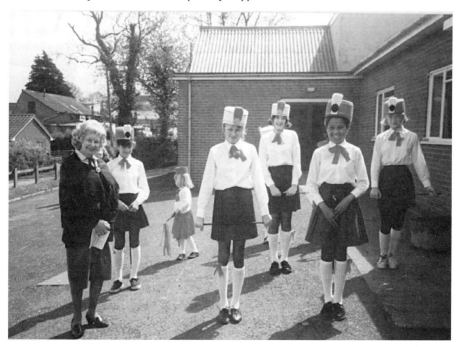

The Speedway Star

Tedburn has its own speedway star. Francis Cann rode for the highly successful Exeter Falcons in the Provincial League during the 1960s, but he was a motorbike enthusiast long before that. In February 1951, whilst in the Army, he won the 350cc class trophy for road racing, a cup which remains a cherished possession. Despite the passing of half a century, he still owns a couple of 1930s motorcycles (a Calthorpe 1932 and a Rudge 1937), which he regularly rides on club or private runs. Top right shows Francis in action, racing around the first bend at the County Ground in Exeter; below, the venue is Newton St Cyres.

The Recreation Ground

In the early part of 1977, a committee was formed and a constitution drawn up with the intention of purchasing land for a recreation field where the village could play football, cricket, tennis and other games. The first members were Harold and Doreen Stacey, R. and T. Matthews, J. Welsh, C. Risdon and D. Burden. The field was purchased from E. and P. Bromell in late 1980.

The first committee meeting after the purchase was held on 6 January 1981. The next step was to address the problem of sorting out access, drainage and fencing around the perimeter.

In November 1983, 250 trees and bushes, which were donated, were planted around the banks surrounding the field. Over the following years, tennis courts and a children's play area were added. The club house and changing rooms were finally added to complete the facilities.

This was a project started by a few enthusiastic people. With fund-raising and grants, and a huge amount of work, the Sports and Recreation Association was formed for the enjoyment of all.

Tedburn's Organisations

It is worth recording the current activities in which Tedburn's residents are engaged. Apologies are extended to any which I have missed out. The long list includes: Football Club, Badminton Club, Cricket Club, Tennis Club, Keep Fit, Women's Institute, Parish Church, Methodist Church, Young Farmers, Art Group, Pre-School, Parent & Toddler Group, Guides, Brownies, Cubs and Scouts, Bingo, Whist Drives, Bonfire and Firework Committee, Fair and Sports Committee, Drama Group, Friendly Friday Group, Outreach and Riding Club. And so it all goes on…

Here we have a picture from George V's Silver Jubilee celebrations of 1935. 'The Tedburn Lads' dressed up for this fun event. Jim Shilston recalls the people in the picture. Back row: C. Bromell, Fred Fry, Stanley Miller, F. Snell, S. Hooper, C. Northcott and C. Bolt. Third row: Jim Shilston, (unknown), D. Bowes, John Wroth, (unknown) and H. Leworthy. Second row: A. Pike, H. Bolt, (unknown), (unknown), I. Knott, (unknown) and J. Taylor. Front row: Bert Miller, D. Gooding, H. Parsons and Sid Bromell.

The excellent picture above features the members of Tedburn St Mary's Young Farmers' Club of 1956.

Below, the Tedburn St Mary group of the Women's Institute had a strong membership when they posed in 1968.

The Millennium Celebrations

The story of Tedburn is now almost up to date. The village celebrated the Millennium in style with a four-day event, which commenced on Friday, 31 December 1999 with a family party and disco. The lighting of candles and a short prayer by Canon J. Tutton were followed by a Grand Firework Display. Local children were presented with commemorative mugs on New Year's Day and a special Millennium Cake was baked. As the next day was a Sunday, a Family United Church Service was held in the Hall and followed by afternoon tea.

The festivities were completed on the Bank Holiday Monday. An exhibition of village history and memorabilia was staged in the John Bromell Room in the morning, whilst 'Costume Through the Ages', a joint venture by the Drama Group and the Women's Institute, was presented that evening.

There is still employment in and around the village (which has a population of about 1,500) including the Village Stores, Post Office, King's Arms Inn, Red Lion Inn, Tedburn Garage, Fry's Agricultural Engineering, Haydens and Fingle Glen Golf Club, civil engineers, builders, thatchers, surveyors, a donkey sanctuary, a milkman, chicken farmers, an organic farm, hairdressers, painters, vets, doctors – and, as telecommunications have improved, there are a number of private home-based businesses.

For the older generation of folks who wish to remain in the village, there is the Tremlett's sheltered housing scheme.

Memories of Peter and his van

Tedburn's Future

As we reach the end of this first history of Tedburn, looking back from the latter half of 2001, we must consider what the future will hold for this small rural village. We see the staple industry of agriculture in crisis, together with increased pressure to build even more houses on this 'green and pleasant land'.

I think that the village's irrepressible community spirit, so much in evidence throughout good times and bad, will see it through. The people of Tedburn are well known for their determination to survive. Today there seems to be a healthy balance between old villagers and new, which bodes well. As we have already seen, instead of the more traditional occupations there are new forms of employment like the ones listed above.

Also on the plus side, at the end of the summer term of 2001 the County Primary School had four classes with over a hundred pupils on the roll.

Let me therefore conclude by saying that I believe Tedburn has got not only a fascinating and varied history but also, hopefully, a prosperous future!